Wildlife Challenge

All things are bound together. All things connect.

What happens to the Earth happens to the children of the Earth.

Man has not woven the web of life. He is but one thread.

Whatever he does to the web, he does to himself.

   Author unknown

Become involved in your world and help save it by supporting your local conservation organizations. The future of our world is in our hands.

Wildlife Challenge

An entertaining and informative game book designed to educate the reader about wildlife and the environment.

Written by Lucy Moreland
Illustrated by Robin D'Alanno
Layout by Beverly Flener

August House Publishers, Inc.

LITTLE ROCK

Concept and text © 1992 by Lucy Moreland. Illustrations © 1992 by Robin D'Alanno.
All rights reserved.

10 9 8 7 6 5 4 3 2 1

LIBRARY OF CONGRESS CATALOGING-IN-PUBLICATION DATA
Moreland, Lucy, 1954—
Wildlife Challenge: an environmental awareness activity for ages 5 to 10 / Lucy Moreland;
illustrations by Robin D'Alanno.
p.   cm.
Summary: Multiple-choice questions in a game format introduce information about animals
and plants in the wild and increase environmental awareness.
ISBN 0-87483-255-1 (pbk.): $9.95
1. Nature study—Juvenile literature. 2. Zoology—Juvenile literature. 3. Education,
Primary—Activity programs—Juvenile literature. [1. Animals—Miscellanea.
2. Plants—Miscellanea. 3. Nature study—Miscellanea.
4. Games.] I. D'Alanno, Robin.
1953— ill. II. Title.
LB1532.M58 1992
372.3'57—dc20   92-19514
.CIP
AC

Printed on archival-quality paper

ACKNOWLEDGEMENTS

The author would like to gratefully acknowledge the following people who contributed to the development of this work.

Special thanks to :   Neil Curry
                      Robin D'Alanno
                      Beverly Flener
                      Carol Griffee
                      Renda Johnston
                      To all of my friends who shared their confidence in my dream.

Cover Photo Credit: Robert Lashley

About the cover:
        Leah, Sarah and Jessica Finn enjoy lunch with little Gizzmo and Bart, the Beavers.

I would like to thank all the people who have made the pieces of this book come together. For my husband's support and encouragement and my children's interest and love of nature.

CONTENTS

INTRODUCTION

Wildlife Challenge was written to educate the growing number of nature enthusiasts who have a real curiosity in discovering the plants and animals that share the world with us. It is hoped that this book provides the spark that lights the flame to a lifetime of awareness of the sensitive habitat we call home.

CATEGORIES

1. *Wildlife Around the World* – Questions in this category relate to animals around the world.

2. *North American Wildlife* – Questions in this category relate to the animals native to North America.

3. *Plants* – Questions in this category relate to the plants that grow in North America and around the world.

4. *Reptiles and Amphibians* – Questions in this category relate to reptiles and amphibians throughout the world.

5. *Birds and Insects* – Questions in this category relate to birds and insects troughout the world.

6. *Information and Facts Around the World* – This category contains questions regarding general information and amazing facts throughout the world.

Wildlife Challenge©

Questions

1. (5) What is a pangolin?
   - A. A raccoon
   - B. An anteater
   - C. A kangaroo

2. (5) The armadillo has poor tolerance for:
   - A. Humidity
   - B. Heat
   - C. Cold

3. (5) The koala's diet consists of two or three pounds of _____ leaves daily.
   - A. Eucalyptus
   - B. Gum
   - C. Banana

4. (5) The most unusual feature about the Southern African Rain Frog is that:
   - A. It spends its entire life under water.
   - B. It does not jump or swim.
   - C. It lives its entire life without eating.

5. (1) True/False

   A penguin is not a bird; it is a mammal.

6. (1) True/False

   The highest mountain is Mt. Everest.

1

Wildlife Challenge©

1. B. An anteater
2. C. Cold
3. A. Eucalyptus
4. B. It does not jump or swim.
5. False
6. True

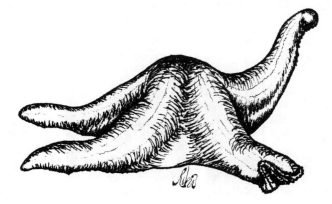

Wildlife Challenge©

Questions

1. (5) The world's largest frog lives in West Africa, weighs up to 6 1/2 pounds, and stretches 2 1/2 feet in length. What is the name of this frog?

   A. Leopard frog
   B. Goliath frog
   C. Bullfrog

2. (1) True/False

   The Nine-banded Armadillo is the only North American mammal with a hard, bony plated shell.

3. (1) True/False

   Deciduous trees are broad-leaved trees that lose their leaves every five years.

4. (5) The record length of the American Alligator is:

   A. 19 feet 2 inches
   B. 29 feet 5 inches
   C. 38 feet 1 inch

5. (5) Dung beetles bury dung by rolling it into a ball and storing it in a safe place. What is dung?

   A. Mushrooms
   B. Animal waste
   C. Decaying roots

6. (5) When only a small number of a specific species are living, they are considered:

   A. Extinct
   B. Biodegradable
   C. Endangered

Wildlife Challenge©

Answers

1. B. Goliath frog
2. True
3. False
4. A. 19 feet 2 inches
5. B. Animal waste
6. C. Endangered

Wildlife Challenge©

Questions

1. (5) How does the Paradise Tree Snake from Southeast Asia return to the ground from the top of a tall tree?
   A. Spirals its body around the tree.
   B. Uses the limbs as steps.
   C. Jumps out and glides down.

2. (5) The North American species of the armadillo is encircled with how many movable bands or rings?
   A. Five
   B. Nine
   C. 12

3. (1) True/False
   Small spiders can be carried a thousand miles by the wind on silken parachutes.

4. (5) Turtles live on every continent except this one:
   A. Arctic
   B. Antarctica
   C. Australia

5. (5) What physical characteristics do some bats and hummingbirds have in common?
   A. Feet
   B. Tongues
   C. Rate of heartbeat

6. (5) Animals that eat other animals as well as plants are called:
   A. Omnivores
   B. Herbivores
   C. Carnivores

5

Wildlife Challenge©

Answers

1. C. Jumps out and glides down.

2. B. Nine

3. True

4. B. Antarctica

5. B. Tongues

6. A. Omnivores

Wildlife Challenge©

Questions

1. (1) True/False

   An adult elephant needs to eat 300 pounds of plants a day.

2. (5) Which of these make up 90 percent of an armadillo's diet?
   A. Invertebrates (bugs, worms, spiders, etc.)
   B. Birds and their eggs
   C. Grass, roots, and tree bark

3. (1) True/False

   Bees take pollen back to their hives by carrying it in a special pouch in their mouths.

4. (5) Which is the fastest swimmer?
   A. Dolphins
   B. Seals
   C. Sailfish

5. (5) A Bob-white Quail builds its nest:
   A. On the ground
   B. In a tree
   C. In a cavity of a dead tree

6. (5) This is a treeless wetland:
   A. Swamp
   B. Marsh
   C. Plain

Wildlife Challenge©

Answers

1. True

2. A. Invertebrates (bugs, worms, spiders, etc.)

3. False

4. C. Sailfish

5. A. On the ground

6. B. Marsh

Wildlife Challenge©

Questions

1. (1) True/False

   The wandering albatross has a wingspan of almost 24 feet.

2. (5) Which answer is incorrect? An armadillo crosses a stream or small body of water by:

   A. Floating across on a stick or log large enough to support it.
   B. Holding its breath and walking on the bottom.
   C. Filling its lungs with air and slowly swimming across.

3. (5) The giant Saguaro Cactus lives to be 200 years old, grows more than 50 feet high, and weighs about 11 tons. What makes up the weight of the cactus?

   A. Heavy, sharp spines
   B. Water in the stems
   C. A vast root system

4. (1) True/False

   The spadefoot toad digs as deep as 10 feet below the desert surface to escape the heat.

5. (5) The male grouse is called a:

   A. Rooster
   B. Cock
   C. Gobbler

6. (5) Considering weight and size, what is the largest living thing?

   A. A tree
   B. A mammal
   C. A fish

9

Wildlife Challenge©

Answers

1. False

2. A. Floating across on a stick or log large enough to support it.

3. B. Water in the stems

4. True

5. B. Cock

6. A. A tree

10

Wildlife Challenge©

Questions

1. (5) The flying dragons that live in Southeast Asia are not really dragons. They are:

    A. Birds
    B. Lizards
    C. Squirrels

2. (1) True/False

    A squirrel uses its tail as a blanket to help it stay warm in the winter and as shade to keep it cool in the summer.

3. (5) The largest flower in the world is the Rafflesia, which grows up to 39 inches across and will weigh:

    A. 8 pounds
    B. 10 pounds
    C. 15 pounds

4. (5) The world's most poisonous fish has 13 large spines that will shoot a deadly poison into anyone who steps on it. An individual who receives a large amount of the poison usually dies within six hours. What is the name of this fish?

    A. Sea horse
    B. Stonefish
    C. Jellyfish

5. (5) A turkey hen builds her nest:

    A. In a tree
    B. On the ground
    C. In a short shrub

6. (5) During the fall of 1822 in Ohio, mass migrations of nearly a quarter of a million of these animals traveled in advancing fronts 100 miles wide, and required five days to pass one area. What were these animals?

    A. Skunks
    B. Gray squirrels
    C. Lemmings

Wildlife Challenge©

Answers

1. B. Lizards
2. True
3. C. 15 pounds
4. B. Stonefish
5. B. On the ground
6. B. Gray squirrels

Wildlife Challenge©

Questions

1. (5) The koala is a:
   A. Marsupial
   B. Rodent
   C. Primate

2. (1) True/False

   Gray squirrels are nocturnal.

3. (5) Carbon dioxide gas enters the leaves of a plant through hundreds of tiny holes called:
   A. Stomata
   B. Chlorophyll
   C. Photosynthesis

4. (5) A newborn American Alligator:
   A. Nurses milk from its mother.
   B. Eats grass and seeds.
   C. Eats insects and crustaceans.

5. (1) True/False

   Hummingbirds are the smallest of North American birds.

6. (5) When water evaporates from the earth's surface, its molecules form a gas known as:
   A. Water vapor
   B. Carbon dioxide
   C. Acid rain

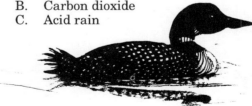

Wildlife Challenge©

Answers

1. A. Marsupial
2. False
3. A. Stomata
4. C. Eats insects and crustaceans.
5. True
6. A. Water vapor

Wildlife Challenge©

Questions

1. (5) How often does the female koala breed?

   A. Once every two years.
   B. Once every five years.
   C. Once every year.

2. (1) True/False

   A gray squirrel depends on memory when it returns to find a previously buried nut.

3. (1) True/False

   A Venus flytrap can catch a small frog.

4. (5) Each year, a Pine snake lays her eggs in the same:

   A. Tree
   B. Burrow
   C. Cave

5. (5) A wood duck builds its nest:

   A. On the ground.
   B. In a burrow of a bank or bluff.
   C. Above ground in the cavity of a tree or stump.

6. (5) What man-made pollution problem has caused about 10,000 lakes in Scandinavia to become devoid of fish, and an equal number of lakes to be threatened?

   A. Acid rain
   B. Oil spills
   C. Raw sewage

Wildlife Challenge©

Answers

1. A. Once every two years

2. False

3. True

4. B. Burrow

5. C. Above ground in the cavity of a tree or stump.

6. A. Acid rain

Wildlife Challenge©

Questions

1. (1) True/False

    The North American Least Shrew is the smallest mammal in the world.

2. (5) The female squirrel gives birth to a litter of three to five tiny youngsters about how many days after being bred?

    A. 10
    B 15
    C. 44

3. (5) Why do the leaves of the giant water lilies float?

    A. There is oil on the leaves.
    B. The leaves are lighter than water.
    C. There are air pockets under the leaves.

4. (5) The diet of the Common Snapping Turtle classifies it as:

    A. A herbivore (eats only plants)
    B. A carnivore (eats only meat and carrion)
    C. An omnivore (eats plants, animals, and carrion)

5. (5) What is a large group of quail called?

    A. A flock
    B. A covey
    C. A clutch

6. (1) True/False

    The United States emits about 30 million tons of sulfur oxide into the atmosphere each year.

Wildlife Challenge©

Answers

1. False

2. C. 44

3. C. Air pockets under the leaves

4. C. An omnivore (eats plants, animals, and carrion)

5. C. A covey

6. True

Wildlife Challenge©

Questions

1. (5) The hump on a camel's back consists of:
   A. Fat
   B. Water
   C. Muscle

2. (1) True/False

   Gray squirrels eat insects, baby birds, and eggs, along with their usual diet of nuts, fruits and seeds.

3. (5) Most of the oxygen in the atmosphere has been produced by:
   A. Animals
   B. Plants
   C. Water

4. (1) True/False

   Snakes are cold-blooded animals and will die if they get too cold, but they can withstand heat temperatures up to 170° F with no ill effects.

5. (5) What predator wraps its prey in bands of silk, dribbles digestive juices onto it, then sucks up the dissolved remains?
   A. Silkworm
   B. Spider
   C. Mud wasp

6. (5) What natural force created beautiful Lake Tahoe in Nevada?
   A. Glaciers
   B. Movements in the earth's crust
   C. The crater of an extinct volcano

19

Wildlife Challenge©

Answers

1. A. Fat

2. True

3. B. Plants

4. False

5. B. Spider

6. C. The crater of an extinct volcano

Wildlife Challenge©

Questions

1. (1) True/False

   Both koala parents raise their young.

2. (1) True/False

   A gray squirrel can smell a nut buried under a foot of snow.

3. (5) Which insects become such a nuisance that caribou will sometimes stand in the sea to get away from them?

   A. Leeches
   B. Ticks
   C. Mosquitoes

4. (5) Which state has eleven kinds of rattlesnakes, more than any other in the United States?

   A. Florida
   B. Texas
   C. Arizona

5. (5) The common name for a Rock Dove is:

   A. Mourning dove
   B. Pigeon
   C. Quail

6. (5) Oregon's Crater Lake was created by:

   A. A collapsed volcano
   B. A glacier
   C. Man

21

Wildlife Challenge©

Answers

1. False

2. True

3. C. Mosquitoes

4. C. Arizona

5. B. Pigeon

6. A. A collapsed volcano

Wildlife Challenge©

Questions

1. (1) True/False

   The world's largest lizard is the Komodo dragon.

2. (1) True/False

   Gray squirrels are true hibernators.

3. (1) True/False

   Only the male glowworm can produce light.

4. (5) How many different kinds of rattlesnakes are found in the United States?

   A. 21
   B. 15
   C. 18

5. (5) A Belted Kingfisher catches its food by:

   A. Diving into the water or close to the surface of the water.
   B. Digging in a tree trunk.
   C. Walking along the bank of a river or pond.

6. (1) True/False

   Sound travels faster through air than it does through water.

Wildlife Challenge©

Answers

1. True

2. False

3. False

4. B.   15

5. A.   Diving into the water or close to the surface of the water.

6. False

Wildlife Challenge©

Questions

1. (5) Approximately how long is an adult giant anteater's tongue?
   - A. 23 inches
   - B. 40 inches
   - C. 38 inches

2. (1) True/False

   A mother gray squirrel will bring nuts and fruits to the nest to feed her young.

3. (5) Acorns make up a large portion of the gray squirrel's diet. Which acorn provides the greatest amount of energy for the squirrel when eaten?
   - A. Red Oak
   - B. White Oak
   - C. Pine Cone

4. (5) When an alligator is basking, it is:
   - A. Submerged in water waiting for prey.
   - B. Mating.
   - C. Lying in the sun.

5. (1) True/False

   Loons are expert divers.

6. (5) What mammals produce the loudest sound of any animal and can be heard 525 miles away?
   - A. Blue Whales
   - B. Dolphins
   - C. Bats

Wildlife Challenge©

Answers

1. A.   23 inches

2. False

3. A.   Red Oak

4. C.   Lying in the sun.

5. True

6. A.   Blue Whales

Wildlife Challenge©

Questions

1. (1) True/False

   Sperm whales may dive to depths greater than 9,000 feet when hunting.

2. (5) The skunk's Latin name is *Mephitis mephitis*. What does Mephitis mean in Latin?

   A. Potent Potion
   B. Noxious Gas
   C. Ready, Aim, Fire

3. (1) True/False

   Cactus roots grow deep into the desert floor.

4. (5) What state has the most incidents of poisonous snake bites?

   A. Georgia
   B. North Carolina
   C. Mississippi

5. (5) A Katydid is really a:

   A. Cricket
   B. Grasshopper
   C. Cicada

6. (5) When hibernating mammals curl up into a ball while they sleep, this spherical shape:

   A. Causes them to lose less body heat.
   B. Takes up less space in the den.
   C. Is more comfortable.

27

Wildlife Challenge©

Answers

1. True

2. B.   Noxious Gas

3. False

4. B.   North Carolina

5. A.   Cricket

6. A.   Causes them to lose less body heat.

Wildlife Challenge©

Questions

1. (5) Which is the largest seal in the Arctic?
   - A. Hooded Seal
   - B. Harp Seal
   - C. Sea Lion

2. (5) The Striped Skunk goes through three warnings before spraying. What is the order of the warnings?
   - A. Hisses and snarls, wheels in a circle, tail raised.
   - B. Charges, retreats, aims and fires.
   - C. Stamps feet, raises tail, turns head to aim.

3. (1) True/False

   Every year, plants trap nearly 28 trillion tons of carbon from carbon dioxide gas and turn it into living material.

4. (5) If attacked, which of the following animal will open its mouth, hiss, bite, and even eject blood from the corners of its eyes?
   - A. Desert Iguana
   - B. Horned Toad (lizard)
   - C. Eastern Fence Lizard

5. (5) A Bombardier beetle repels a predator by:
   - A. Spraying a boiling chemical liquid.
   - B. Dipping and diving, evading his attacker in mid air.
   - C. Dropping small rocks from the air.

6. (5) North America has _____ distinct deserts.
   - A. Four
   - B. Six
   - C. Three

Wildlife Challenge©

Answers

1.   A.   Hooded Seal

2.   C.   Stamps feet, raises tail, turns head to aim.

3.   True

4.   B.   Horned Toad (lizard)

5.   A.   Spraying a boiling chemical liquid.

6.   A.   Four

Wildlife Challenge©

Questions

1. (5) Half of the caribou's diet is made up of reindeer moss or gray lichen that provides them with a unique protection. The moss produces:

   A. A protein that gives them excellent eyesight.
   B. An anti-freeze that allows the caribou to endure below-freezing temperatures.
   C. A strong odor that detours mosquitoes and other annoying insects.

2. (1) True/False

   If necessary, a skunk can spray five or six consecutive rounds of musk, with each dose being a mere fraction of a teaspoon.

3. (5) A cypress tree grows:

   A. In shallow water

   B. In the desert
   C. On steep slopes of mountain ranges.

4. (5) What six-foot-long fish goes into hibernation during hot seasons and can live up to four years without food or water?

   A. Stonefish
   B. Lungfish
   C. Catfish

5. (5) Dragonflies lay their eggs:

   A. Buried beneath tree bark
   B. In water
   C. In the roots of grasses

6. (5) The North American desert with the highest altitude is:

   A. The Great Basin
   B. The Mojave Desert
   C. The Sonora Desert

31

Wildlife Challenge©

Answers

1. B. An anti-freeze that allows the caribou to endure below-freezing temperatures.

2. True

3. A. In shallow water

4. B. Lungfish

5. B. In water

6. A. The Great Basin

Wildlife Challenge©

Questions

1. (5) The spiral tusk protruding from the head of a narwhal is a:
   A. Tooth
   B. Horn
   C. Bone

2. (1) True/False

   A skunk can only spray its musk one time within 25 minutes.

3. (5) A fern's rhizomes are like its:
   A. Leaves
   B. Roots
   C. Flowers

4. (5) A toad can flick its tongue out and back in:
   A. 1/2 of a second
   B. 1/4 of a second
   C. 1/14 of a second

5. (5) Which state is called the Pelican State?
   A. Louisiana
   B. Alabama
   C. Mississippi

6. (5) True/False

   All mammals are cold-blooded.

Wildlife Challenge©

Answers

1. A. Tooth
2. False
3. B. Roots
4. C. 1/14 of a second
5. A. Louisiana
6. False

Wildlife Challenge©

Questions

1. (1) Does a whale's tail move from side to side or up and down while swimming?

2. (5) Skunks are members of which family?
   A. Squirrel
   B. Weasel
   C. Rodent

3. (5) Originally, the troublesome weed Johnson Grass was imported from _____ as an experiment for use in hay crops.
   A. Korea
   B. Turkey
   C. Africa

4. (3) All pit vipers have:
   A. Round pupils
   B. Horizontal pupils
   C. Vertical pupils

5. (5) Which of the following birds does not fly south for the winter?
   A. Swift
   B. Hummingbird
   C. Whip-poor-will

6. (5) During the 1800s skunk musk was occasionally used to treat this illness:
   A. Smallpox
   B. Asthma
   C. Gout

1. Up and down
2. B. Weasel
3. B. Turkey
4. C. Vertical pupils
5. C. Whip-poor-will
6. B. Asthma

Wildlife Challenge©

Questions

1. (5) The world's largest rodent is the:
   - A. North American Beaver
   - B. South American Capabara
   - C. Red Kangaroo of Australia

2. (1) Which has the most offensive and strong musk — a Spotted Skunk or a Striped Skunk?

3. (1) True/False

   Deciduous trees are broad-leaved trees that lose their leaves in the winter.

4. (5) The Portuguese man-of-war is a:
   - A. Octopus
   - B. Jellyfish
   - C. Sponge

5. (5) Why do desert beetles stand on their heads in the Namid Desert of Southwest Africa?
   - A. To protect themselves from the sun.
   - B. So the fog can condense onto their bodies and trickle down into their mouths for an easy drink.
   - C. This position makes them look like small cacti to predators.

6. (5) The term "cold-blooded" means the body temperature:
   - A. Is below 70°
   - B. Changes with the surrounding temperature
   - C. Is below 60°

37

Wildlife Challenge©

Answers

1. B.   South American Capabara

2.   The Spotted Skunk

3.   True

4. B.   Jellyfish

5. B.   So the fog can condense onto their bodies
         and trickle down into their mouths
         for an easy drink.

6. B.   Changes with the surrounding
         temperature.

Wildlife Challenge©

Questions

1. (5) What is the name of the whale that has a spiral tusk 12 feet long protruding from the upper lip of its mouth?
   A. Orca whale
   B. Pilot whale
   C. Narwhal

2. (5) Baby skunks are called:
   A. Pups
   B. Kittens
   C. Kits

3. (5) Spanish Moss and Bunchmoss grow:
   A. In trees
   B. In caves
   C. On the ground

4. (5) Of the three lizards named below, which one is not venomous?
   A. Texas Horned Lizard
   B. Gila monster
   C. Beaded Lizard

5. (5) The osprey's diet is made up mostly of:
   A. Small rodents
   B. Fish
   C. Dead animals

6. (5) Animals that eat other animals are called:
   A. Omnivores
   B. Herbivores
   C. Carnivores

Wildlife Challenge©

1. C. Narwhal
2. C. Kits
3. A. In trees
4. A. Texas Horned Lizard
5. B. Fish
6. C. Carnivores

Wildlife Challenge©

Questions

1. (1) True/False

   The Blue Whale will eat 11 tons of shrimp in one meal.

2. (1) True/False

   At birth, a baby skunk's eyes and ears are open.

3. (5) Spanish Moss is a member of which family?
   A. Fungi
   B. Fern
   C. Pineapple

4. (5) A worm snake is called a worm snake because it:
   A. Has no eyes and looks like a worm.
   B. Eats only earthworms.
   C. Is a worm and not a snake.

5. (5) Grebe chicks will ride piggyback while their parent:
   A. Flies from danger.
   B. Dives underwater for food.
   C. Fights to protect its territory.

6. (5) The deepest freshwater lake in the world is 5,315 feet deep and contains 1/5th of the world's fresh water. Lake Baikal is located in:
   A. Russia
   B. Scotland
   C. Africa

41

Wildlife Challenge©

Answers

1. True

2. False

3. C. Pineapple

4. B. Eats only earthworms.

5. B. Dives underwater for food.

6. A. Russia

Wildlife Challenge©

Questions

1. (5) The narwhal, sometimes known as the Unicorn of the Sea, has _____ teeth.
   - A. Two
   - B. 24
   - C. Six

2. (1) True/False

   A two-day-old baby skunk can use its musk glands to spray an intruder entering its nest.

3. (5) A Prickly Pear is a:
   - A. Tree
   - B. Shrub
   - C. Cactus

4. (1) True/False

   If a rattlesnake loses or damages its fangs, it will die of starvation.

5. (5) How many legs does a spider have?
   - A. Four
   - B. Six
   - C. Eight

6. (5) Because this animal kept insects, mice, moles, and shrews out of the hop fields, New York state legislators passed a bill to protect it. Name this animal.
   - A. Armadillo
   - B. Opossum
   - C. Skunk

Wildlife Challenge©

Answers

1. A. Two
2. False
3. C. Cactus
4. False
5. C. Eight
6. C. Skunk

Wildlife Challenge©

Questions

1. (5) Hippopotamus is a Greek word that means:
   - A. Large mouth
   - B. Amphibious
   - C. River horse

2. (5) What is the greatest natural predator of the skunk?
   - A. Coyote
   - B. Bear
   - C. Great Horned Owl

3. (5) Poison Ivy is a:
   - A. Vine or ground cover
   - B. Shrub
   - C. Tree

4. (5) Which reptile is more abundant in the United States?
   - A. The American Alligator
   - B. The American Crocodile
   - C. The Spectacle Caniman

5. (5) Male mosquitoes feed on:
   - A. Blood
   - B. Nectar
   - C. Nothing at all

6. (5) In the western United States, what long, high ridge makes the Continental Divide?
   - A. Smoky Mountains
   - B. Rocky Mountains
   - C. Grand Canyon

Wildlife Challenge©

Answers

1. C. River horse

2. C. Great Horned Owl

3. A. Vine or ground cover

4. A. The American Alligator

5. B. Nectar

6. B. Rocky Mountains

Wildlife Challenge©

Questions

1. (5) Because of the richness of its mother's milk, this seal is only four days old when it is totally weaned.
   - A. Harp Seal
   - B. Leopard Seal
   - C. Hooded Seal

2. (1) True/False

   The Spotted Skunk does a handstand on its front paws before it sprays.

3. (5) Which of the following is without chlorophyll and therefore cannot manufacture its own food from water, air, and soil minerals?
   - A. Wild rice
   - B. Mushrooms
   - C. Persimmons

4. (1) True/False

   Dried rattlesnake poison (venom) keeps its deadly strength for at least 50 years, and probably longer.

5. (5) The Belted Kingfisher makes its nest:
   - A. In a tree cavity
   - B. By tunneling in a steep bank
   - C. On the ground near water

6. (5) In which region does the cassowary, Red Kangaroo, kiwi and koala live?
   - A. South American
   - B. African
   - C. Australian

47

Wildlife Challenge©

Answers

1. C. Hooded Seal

2. True

3. B. Mushrooms

4. True

5. B. By tunneling in a steep bank

6. C. Australian

Wildlife Challenge©

Questions

1. (5) Because of the climate, this is the only state in the United States where koalas can be kept in zoos:
   A. Florida
   B. Arizona
   C. California

2. (1) True/False

   The average weight of a White-tailed Deer is from 300 to 450 pounds.

3. (1) True/False

   It takes more than 500,000 trees to make the newspapers Americans read on one Sunday.

4. (1) True/False

   A rattlesnake can only strike its victim from a coiled position.

5. (5) A male turkey is called a:
   A. Cock
   B. Rooster
   C. Gobbler

6. (5) The coldest desert in North America is:
   A. The Mojave
   B. The Great Basin
   C. Death Valley

49

Wildlife Challenge©

1. C. California

2. False

3. True

4. False

5. C. Gobbler

6. B. The Great Basin

Wildlife Challenge©

Questions

1. (5) Even though ostriches have small brains, they have been trained to:
    A. Catch fish in shallow pools
    B. Herd sheep
    C. Fly

2. (5) The White-tailed Deer buck's antlers are covered with a soft, tender membrane that can be injured easily. What is this covering called?
    A. Rack
    B. Fleece
    C. Velvet

3. (5) According to the Poison Control Centers throughout the United States, what house plant was the cause of more hospitalizations from ingestion (swallowing) than any other in 1974?
    A. Buckeye
    B. Philodendron
    C. Iris

4. (1) True/False

    A rattlesnake does not have to be coiled to strike; it can strike from almost any position.

5. (1) True/False

    Monarch butterflies migrate instead of hibernating.

6. (5) Yes/No

    Do you get a pound of ice from a pound of water?

Wildlife Challenge©

Answers

1. B. Herd sheep

2. C. Velvet

3. B. Philodendron

4. True

5. True

6. Yes

Wildlife Challenge©

Questions

1. (5) How does the anteater grind the thousands of ants and termites it eats each day?
   - A. With hundreds of small teeth.
   - B. Crushes them with its rough tongue.
   - C. Swallows them and lets its powerful stomach muscles grind them.

2. (5) If a buck White-tailed Deer stamps his front feet and waves his antlers at you, this is a sign that he is:
   - A. Afraid
   - B. Ready to attack
   - C. Looking for a place to hide

3. (1) True/False

   The leaves and berries of mistletoe are very poisonous.

4. (5) Snakes eat:
   - A. Plants
   - B. Animals
   - C. Both plants and animals

5. (1) True/False

   Heat is given off by the lights that fireflies and glowworms produce.

6. (5) What is the fastest land animal?
   - A. Cheetah
   - B. Spring Buck
   - C. Pronghorn

Wildlife Challenge©

Answers

1. C.   Swallows them and lets its powerful
         stomach muscles grind them.

2. B.   Ready to attack

3. True

4. B.   Animals

5. False

6. A.   Cheetah

Wildlife Challenge©

Questions

1. (5) A penguin is a:
   - A. Seal
   - B. Bird
   - C. Mammal

2. (1) True/False

   The White-tailed Deer can see the colors red, blue, green, and yellow.

3. (5) Mistletoe is a plant that grows:
   - A. On the ground
   - B. On the limbs of hardwood trees
   - C. In shallow water

4. (1) True/False

   A snake's meal is always swallowed whole.

5. (1) True/False

   A Chuckar is a large partridge that was introduced into the western part of the United States.

6. (5) What is the difference between a swamp and a marsh?
   - A. Mammals are not present in swamps, but are present in marshes.
   - B. A swamp has trees, but a marsh does not.
   - C. A swamp drains from south to north; a marsh drains from north to south.

Wildlife Challenge©

Answers

1. B. Bird

2. False

3. B. On the limbs of hardwood trees

4. True

5. True

6. A. A swamp has trees; a marsh does not.

Wildlife Challenge©

Questions

1. (1) True/False

   In the Amazon River, there are fish with four eyes.

2. (1) True/False

   Before man populated the U.S., the White-tailed Deer was preyed upon by the mountain lion and wolf. Now that the mountain lion and wolf are endangered, hunting seasons are used to manage deer populations.

3. (1) True/False

   The entire plant of the azalea is poisonous.

4. (5) Snakes always swallow their prey:

   A. Head first
   B. Tail first
   C. By chewing it in little pieces.

5. (5) Which bird holds the record for the longest flight migration from the North Pole to the South Pole, and back again to the North Pole?

   A. Emperor Penguin
   B. Arctic Tern
   C. Bar-headed Goose

6. (5) The hottest land temperature ever recorded was 136° in the:

   A. Sahara Desert
   B. Great Salt Basin
   C. Mojave Desert

Wildlife Challenge©

Answers

1. True

2. True

3. True

4. A. Head first

5. B. Arctic Tern

6. A. Sahara Desert

Wildlife Challenge©

Questions

1. (1) True/False

   To conserve water, a camel will swallow its own nose drippings.

2. (5) What happens to the neck of a buck White-tailed Deer when he goes into rut?

   A. It swells
   B. Becomes taller
   C. Becomes shorter

3. (5) Apple, peach, pear, strawberries, and blackberries are members of what plant family?

   A. Rose family
   B. Elm family
   C. Beech family

4. (1) True/False

   All of the known sea snakes are poisonous.

5. (5) The communicating sounds of grasshoppers, katydids, crickets and cicadas are made by:

   A. Both male and female
   B. Only the male
   C. Only the female

6. (5) Animals that eat plants are called:

   A. Omnivores
   B. Herbivores
   C. Carnivores

Wildlife Challenge©

Answers

1. True
2. A. Swells
3. A. Rose family
4. True
5. B. Only the male
6. B. Herbivores

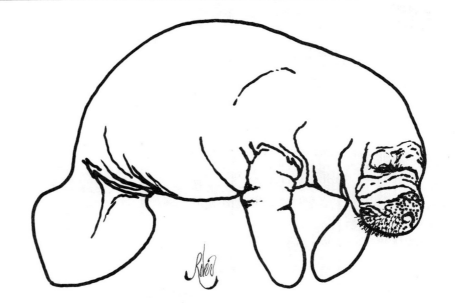

Wildlife Challenge©

Questions

1. (5) Which whale's mouth may make up almost a third of its body?
   A. Sperm Whale
   B. Blue Whale
   C. Bowhead Whale

2. (5) What is the most common hoofed wild animal in North America?
   A. Mule Deer
   B. Moose
   C. White-tailed Deer

3. (5) The weeping willow is native to what country?
   A. United States
   B. China
   C. Australia

4. (1) True/False

   All sea snakes have gills and do not need to surface to breathe.

5. (5) Fireflies use their light to:
   A. Attract a mate
   B. Attract food
   C. See in the dark

6. (5) From what source do all plants receive their energy?
   A. Oceans
   B. Forest
   C. Sun

Wildlife Challenge©

Answers

1. C. Bowhead Whale
2. C. White-tailed Deer
3. B. China
4. False
5. A. Attract a mate
6. C. Sun

Wildlife Challenge©

Questions

1. (1) True/False

   When a camel excretes its feces, the waste is so dry that it can be used to start fires.

2. (1) True/False

   A buck deer grows a new set of antlers every year.

3. (5) The leaves of a sweet gum tree are:
   A. Shaped like a star
   B. Long and narrow
   C. Perfectly round

4. (5) The heaviest snake in the world is the:
   A. Python
   B. Anaconda
   C. Boa

5. (1) True/False

   An owl can move its eyes from side to side and up and down without moving its head.

6. (5) The Finger Lakes in New York were created by:
   A. Ancient volcanoes
   B. Glaciers
   C. A violent earthquake

Wildlife Challenge©

Answers

1. True

2. True

3. A. Shaped like a star

4. B. Anaconda

5. False

6. B. Glaciers

Wildlife Challenge©

Questions

1. (5) At birth, a baby koala is the size of a:
   - A. Lima bean
   - B. Chicken egg
   - C. Domestic kitten

2. (5) The White-tailed Deer fawn has about this number of white spots on its tawny-red coat:
   - A. 100
   - B. 1,000
   - C. 300

3. (5) Mesquite is a:
   - A. Vine
   - B. Tree or shrub
   - C. Grass

4. (1) True/False
   A large Python can swallow an entire goat.

5. (5) This is the smallest falcon in the United States.
   - A. American Kestrel
   - B. Sharp-shinned Hawk
   - C. Peregrine Falcon

6. (5) What river created the Grand Canyon in the United States?
   - A. Red River
   - B. Colorado River
   - C. Rio Grande River

Wildlife Challenge©

Answers

1. A. Lima Bean
2. C. 300
3. B. Tree or shrub
4. True
5. A. American Kestrel
6. B. Colorado River

Wildlife Challenge©

Questions

1. (1) True/False
   Koalas are nocturnal.

2. (5) How does the buck deer remove the velvet covering from his antlers?
   A. By fighting with another buck.
   B. By washing if off in a cold stream.
   C. By rubbing against the trunks of small trees and brush.

3. (5) For thousands of years, the wood of this tree has been the choice for making archers' bows.
   A. Oak
   B. Yew
   C. Dogwood

4. (5) In the jungles of Thailand, the snake with a record length of 33 feet is a:
   A. Python
   B. Anaconda
   C. Boa constrictor

5. (5) Cicadas are related to:
   A. Crickets
   B. Grasshoppers
   C. Aphids

6. (5) In which state is the beginning (source) of the Mississippi River?
   A. Minnesota
   B. Mississippi
   C. North Dakota

Wildlife Challenge©

Answers

1. True

2. C. By rubbing against the trunks of small trees and brush.

3. B. Yew

4. A. Python

5. C. Aphids

6. A. Minnesota

Wildlife Challenge©

Questions

1. (1) True/False

   A Mandrill is a very elusive primate.

2. (1) True/False

   During the early 1900s, the White-tailed Deer was eliminated in much of its range.

3. (5) All parts of this tree are poisonous.
   - A. Pine
   - B. Oak
   - C. Yew

4. (5) What term describes a sensory organ between the eye and nostril on each side of the head of vipers (snakes)?
   - A. Wave
   - B. Pit
   - C. Hollow

5. (1) True/False

   The Common Loon can take flight only from a large body of water.

6. (5) How do biologists determine the age of a White-tailed Deer?
   - A. By the size of its antlers.
   - B. By tooth replacement and wear.
   - C. By the size and wear of its hooves.

Wildlife Challenge©

Answers

1. True

2. True

3. C. Yew

4. B. Pit

5. True

6. B. By tooth replacement and wear

Wildlife Challenge©

Questions

1. (1) True/False

   Only the male giraffe has horns.

2. (5) After a White-tailed Deer doe is bred, birth of fawns will follow in about _____ days.

   A. 65
   B. 105
   C. 205

3. (1) True/False

   The toxic oils of poison ivy and poison oak retain their strength for many years.

4. (5) By using its sense of smell to locate prey, the Texas Blind Snake eats:

   A. Ants and termites
   B. Rats and mice
   C. Eggs of birds

5. (1) True/False

   The Ring-necked Pheasant is an imported bird. It is not a true native bird of North America.

6. (5) In polar regions, what keeps insect eggs, plants, and pupae (larva) from freezing?

   A. They are constantly moving.
   B. They contain a natural antifreeze.
   C. They hibernate.

Wildlife Challenge©

Answers

1. False

2. C.   205

3. True

4. A.   Ants and termites

5. True

6. B.   They contain a natural antifreeze.

Wildlife Challenge©

Questions

1. (5) In 1990, the world's tropical rain forests were being damaged or destroyed at the rate of about:
   A. 100 acres per minute
   B. 5,000 acres per minute
   C. 25,000 acres per minute

2. (1) True/False
   Yearling White-tailed Deer does usually produce a single fawn, but after that, twins are the rule in a healthy herd.

3. (5) In Europe during the 14th century, what precious spice was traded, ounce per ounce, for gold?
   A. Black pepper
   B. Coffee beans
   C. Tea leaves

4. (5) A female alligator:
   A. Lays eggs in a nest made of mud and sticks.
   B. Lays eggs in the bottom of a shallow pool of water.
   C. Gives live birth to up to 50 blind, helpless babies.

5. (5) Which one of these woodpeckers is endangered?
   A. Red-headed Woodpecker
   B. Pileated Woodpecker
   C. Red-cockaded Woodpecker

6. (5) An animal that captures another animal for food is called:
   A. Prey
   B. A scavenger
   C. A predator

Wildlife Challenge©

Answers

1. A. 100 acres per minute
2. True
3. A. Black pepper
4. A. Lays eggs in a nest made of mud and sticks.
5. C. Red-cockaded Woodpecker
6. C. A predator

Wildlife Challenge©

Questions

1. (1) True/False

   A giraffe's horns are covered with skin and hair and are not true horns.

2. (1) True/False

   The newborn White-tailed Deer fawn has no scent to attract predators.

3. (5) Coffee is made from which part of the coffee tree?

   A. Roots
   B. Beans
   C. Leaves

4. (5) Which snake is sometimes called the ground rattler?

   A. Copperhead
   B. Pigmy Rattlesnake
   C. Canebrake Rattlesnake

5. (5) The Common Nighthawk is a nocturnal bird that eats:

   A. Other birds
   B. Small animals
   C. Flying insects

6. (5) Animals that remove and eat dead animals are called:

   A. Predators
   B. Scavengers
   C. Decomposers

Wildlife Challenge©

Answers

1. True

2. True

3. B. Beans

4. B. Pigmy Rattlesnake

5. C. Flying insects

6. B. Scavengers

Wildlife Challenge©

Questions

1. (1) To the Aborigines, or native Australians, what does the word "koala" mean?

   A. "Tree Bear"
   B. "Drinks No Water"
   C. "Tree Eater"

2. (1) True/False

   Antlers are hollow in the center.

3. (5) Cocoa comes from this part of a 40-foot evergreen tree that is native to the tropics of Central and South America.

   A. Roots
   B. Leaves
   C. Beans

4. (1) Yes/No

   Can a cottonmouth (water moccasin) bite under water?

5. (5) The Common Nighthawk is a close relative of the:

   A. Falcon
   B. Whip-poor-will
   C. Hawk

6. (5) If you are a student of Herpetology, you are studying:

   A. Flowers
   B. Trees
   C. Reptiles

Wildlife Challenge©

Answers

1. B. "Drinks No Water"
2. False
3. C. Beans
4. Yes
5. Whip-poor-will
6. C. Reptiles

Wildlife Challenge©

Questions

1. (5) The largest marsupial (pouched mammal) lives in:

   A. Australia
   B. Asia
   C. South America

2. (1) True/False

   A deer is a very poor swimmer because of its thin legs and small feet.

3. (1) Coffee beans contain a natural substance that stimulates the central nervous system. What is this substance called?

   A. Caffeine
   B. Opium
   C. Strychnine

4. (1) True/False

   The Coachwhip is a very poisonous snake.

5. (5) The female ostrich can distinguish her eggs from other ostrich eggs by:

   A. The color of the egg
   B. The size of the egg
   C. The pores in the eggshell

6. (5) If you have Ophidiophobia (O-fid-e-fo-be-a) you have a fear of what?

   A. Spiders
   B. Birds
   C. Snakes

Wildlife Challenge©

Answers

1. A. Australia
2. False
3. A. Caffeine
4. False
5. C. The pores in the eggshell
6. C. Snakes

Wildlife Challenge©

Questions

1. (1) True/False

   The giraffe is the tallest living animal.

2. (5) When a deer raises its tail to expose the white underside, it is telling other deer:

   A. Danger
   B. This is my territory
   C. Food is abundant

3. (5) Strychnine is a poison that is processed from the seeds of:

   A. A dogwood tree
   B. A castor bean
   C. A strychnine tree

4. (1) True/False

   Garter snakes and ribbon snakes lay eggs—they do not give live birth.

5. (5) Which southwest African bird builds a thickly thatched, dome-like communal nest that provides the colony shelter year round?

   A. Weaverbird
   B. Bluejay
   C. Flamingo

6. (5) The ozone layer of the earth's atmosphere:

   A. Blocks out deadly ultraviolet radiation from the sun.
   B. Keeps the water/moisture on the earth's surface from evaporating into outer space.
   C. Helps control the gravitational pull of the sun.

Wildlife Challenge©

Answers

1. True

2. A. Danger

3. C. A Strychnine tree

4. True

5. A. Weaverbird

6. A. Blocks out deadly ultraviolet radiation from the sun.

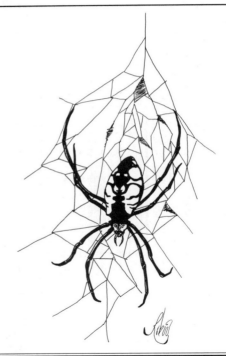

Wildlife Challenge©

Questions

1. (5) What does a muskox herd do when it is approached by predators?
   A. It forms two columns with the young and weak in the center and slowly moves away from danger.
   B. It pushes the old and weak out to the predators as sacrifices.
   C. It forms a circle with heads facing danger and encircles the young for maximum protection.

2. (1) True/False

   The Mule Deer is larger than the White-tailed Deer.

3. (5) The U.S. Food and Drug Administration classified this as a poisonous plant:
   A. Sweet gum
   B. Lily of the Valley
   C. Cornflower

4. (1) True/False

   Geckos are members of the lizard family.

5. (5) This is the smallest hawk/falcon in the United States:
   A. American Kestrel
   B. Sharp-shinned Hawk
   C. The Peregrine Falcon

6. (5) Water covers what percent of the earth's surface?
   A. 42 percent
   B. 50 percent
   C. 70 percent

Wildlife Challenge©

Answers

1. C. It forms a circle with heads facing danger and encircles the young for maximum protection.

2. True

3. B. Lily of the Valley

4. True

5. A. American Kestrel

6. C. 70 percent

Wildlife Challenge©

Questions

1. (1) True/False

    An adult giraffe will consume about 75 pounds of food every 24 hours.

2. (5) What is North America's fastest mammal, running at speeds exceeding 40 miles an hour and covering 20 feet in one leap?

    A. White-tailed Deer
    B. Mule Deer
    C. Pronghorn

3. (5) The Passion Flower grows as:

    A. A tree
    B. A vine
    C. A shrub

4. (5) What turtle has the most widespread population throughout the United States?

    A. Snapping Turtle
    B. Box Turtle
    C. Bog Turtle

5. (5) The Common Flicker is a member of this family:

    A. Crow
    B. Woodpecker
    C. Lark

6. (5) What natural disaster killed more than a quarter of a million people in November 1970?

    A. An earthquake
    B. A hurricane
    C. A volcano

Wildlife Challenge©

Answers

1. True
2. C. Pronghorn
3. B. Vine
4. A. Snapping Turtle
5. B. Woodpecker
6. B. A hurricane

Wildlife Challenge©

Questions

1. (5) The favorite food of a koala is the leaves of these trees:
   A. Pine
   B. Eucalyptus and gum
   C. Sycamore

2. (5) What is a young woodchuck called?
   A. Whip
   B. Pup
   C. Kit

3. (5) Two uses of the bright yellow flowers of dandelions are to make yellow dye and:
   A. Wine
   B. Fingernail polish
   C. Latex paint

4. (1) True/False
   Gila monsters are the world's only venomous lizards.

5. (5) This woodpecker drills holes in the trunks of trees and eats the sap that runs out as well as the insects trapped in it.
   A. Flicker
   B. Gnatcatcher
   C. Yellow-bellied Sapsucker

6. (1) True/False
   A person struck by lightning is usually knocked unconscious and stops breathing.

Wildlife Challenge©

Answers

1. B. Eucalyptus and gum
2. C. Kit
3. A. Wine
4. False
5. C. Yellow-bellied Sapsucker
6. True

Wildlife Challenge©

Questions

1. (5) Each giraffe has a unique color pattern that distinguishes one from another. Where are these color patterns located?

   A. Legs
   B. Head
   C. Neck

2. (5) A groundhog's normal heartbeat is 80 beats per minute. When a groundhog is hibernating, its heart beats about how many times per minute?

   A. Five
   B. 30
   C. 40

3. (1) True/False

   All ferns are classified as flowering plants.

4. (1) True/False

   Alligators of all sizes make a hissing sound.

5. (1) Which bird is larger, the Hairy Woodpecker or the Downy Woodpecker?

6. (1) True/False

   It is possible for a cloud to weigh a ton or more.

Wildlife Challenge©

Answers

1. C. Neck

2. A. Five

3. False

4. True

5. The Hairy Woodpecker

6. True

Wildlife Challenge©

Questions

1. (5) Where do wombats live?
   A. In a tree
   B. Underground
   C. In water

2. (5) When a woodchuck is not in hibernation, it breathes about 2,100 times an hour. How many times an hour does a woodchuck breathe when it is hibernating?
   A. 500
   B. 100
   C. 10

3. (5) Brambles (blackberries, raspberries, and dewberries) are members of this family:
   A. Holly
   B. Rose
   C. Cacti

4. (5) A snake is:
   A. A reptile
   B. An amphibian
   C. An insect

5. (1) True/False

   The very social Acorn Woodpecker has been known to store up to 50,000 acorns in individual holes in a single Ponderosa Pine Tree.

6. (1) True/False

   The longest canyon in the world is the Grand Canyon in Arizona.

Wildlife Challenge©

Answers

1. B. Underground
2. C. 10
3. B. Rose
4. A. Reptile
5. True
6. True

Wildlife Challenge©

Questions

1. (5) These are the only cats that live and hunt together:

   A. Cougars
   B. Lions
   C. Cheetahs

2. (1) True/False

   The eastern cottontail digs a burrow three feet into the ground.

3. (5) Barrel cacti are known as "compass cacti" because they always lean _____.

   A. South
   B. North
   C. West

4. (5) The tongue of a chameleon is:

   A. One-half the length of its body
   B. The length of its body
   C. Twice the length of its body

5. (1) True/False

   Mississippi is known as the Pelican State.

6. (5) What is the shape of every falling raindrop?

   A. Round or oval
   B. Teardrop shaped
   C. They have no specific shape.

Wildlife Challenge©

Answers

1. B. Lions

2. False

3. A. South

4. C. Twice the length of its body

5. False

6. C. They have no specific shape.

Wildlife Challenge©

Questions

1. (5) A family of lions is called a:

   A. Herd
   B. Pride
   C. Pack

2. (1) True/False

   Eastern Cottontail rabbits are born with their eyes sealed shut, and they have very little hair.

3. (5) Only one species of the Ginkgo trees exists today. Ginkgoes are native trees of:

   A. South America
   B. Australia
   C. The Orient

4. (1) True/False

   All fish have eyelids and they sleep with their eyes open.

5. (1) Which pelican sights its prey while in flight, then dives into the water to catch it—the Brown Pelican or the American White Pelican?

6. (5) Tropical cyclones are called hurricanes when wind speeds exceed _____ miles an hour?

   A. 60
   B. 73
   C. 120

Wildlife Challenge©

Answers

1. B. Pride
2. True
3. C. The Orient
4. False
5. The Brown Pelican
6. B. 73

Wildlife Challenge©

Questions

1. (5) Newborn zebras identify their mothers primarily by:
   A. Smell
   B. Sight
   C. Sound

2. (1) True/False

   There are eight different species of rabbits in North America.

3. (5) Carolina Jasmine is the state flower of which state?
   A. North Carolina
   B. South Carolina
   C. Tennessee

4. (5) How often does a new rattle appear on the tail of a rattlesnake?
   A. One rattle for every year
   B. Every time it sheds its skin.
   C. One rattle every two years

5. (5) The _____ does not dive from the air to catch fish.
   A. American White Pelican
   B. Brown Pelican
   C. Belted Kingfisher

6. (5) The second longest river in the world begins as a small stream in the Andes Mountains. What is the name of this river?
   A. Thames River
   B. Rhine River
   C. Amazon River

Wildlife Challenge©

Answers

1. B. Sight

2. True

3. B. South Carolina

4. B. Every time it sheds its skin.

5. A. American White Pelican

6. C. Amazon River

Wildlife Challenge©

Questions

1. (5) Why do camels have long eyelashes?
   A. To keep out the blinding sun.
   B. To prevent moisture from evaporating from their eyes.
   C. To protect their eyes during desert sandstorms.

2. (5) A Cottontail's "form" is where it:
   A. Bathes
   B. Sleeps
   C. Feeds

3. (1) True/False
   A tree has almost as many roots underground as it has branches above the ground.

4. (5) When frightened, this large, timid lizard flees into a rock crevice and inflates its body so that it is wedged into place and a predator cannot pull it out.
   A. Short-horned Lizard
   B. Chuckwallas
   C. Ground Skink

5. (5) When American White Pelicans form a line in the water and swim toward the beach beating their wings, what are they doing?
   A. Fishing
   B. Mating
   C. Driving away enemies

6. (5) Lake Itasca State Park marks the source (beginning) of what river?
   A. Missouri River
   B. Ohio River
   C. Mississippi River

Wildlife Challenge©

Answers

1. C. To protect their eyes during desert
       sandstorms.

2. B. Sleeps

3. True

4. B. Chuckwallas

5. A. Fishing

6. C. Mississippi River

Wildlife Challenge – *Junior Edition*©

Questions

1. (5) What color is a polar bear?

   A. Brown
   B. White
   C. Black

2. (5) A beaver builds its home:

   A. In or near water
   B. In a tree
   C. In the desert sand

3. (1) True/False

   A pine tree is green all year.

4. (1) Yes/No

   If a lizard loses its tail, a new one will grow back.

5. (5) A mosquito is a:

   A. Bird
   B. Mouse
   C. Insect

6. (5) An armadillo makes its home:

   A. In the top of a tree
   B. In a burrow underground
   C. In a pond or lake

Wildlife Challenge – *Junior Edition*©

Answers

1. B. White
2. A. In or near water
3. True
4. Yes
5. C. Insect
6. B. In a burrow underground.

Wildlife Challenge – *Junior Edition*©

Questions

1. (5) A camel lives in the:

   A. Desert
   B. Forest
   C. Ocean

2. (5) A baby bobcat is called a:

   A. Puppy
   B. Chick
   C. Kitten

3. (5) A mushroom is a:

   A. Plant
   B. Animal
   C. Bird

4. (5) Snakes eat:

   A. Mice and birds
   B. Grass and leaves
   C. Fruits and vegetables

5. (5) A bluejay and a crow are:

   A. Cats
   B. Mice
   C. Birds

6. (5) A place where there is very little rainfall is called a:

   A. Rain forest
   B. Desert
   C. Wetland

Wildlife Challenge – *Junior Edition*©

Answers

1. A. Desert
2. C. Kitten
3. A. Plant
4. A. Mice and birds
5. C. Birds
6. B. Desert

Wildlife Challenge – *Junior Edition*©

Questions

1. (5) Which animal is black with two white stripes down its back and smells real bad when you scare him?

    A. A rabbit
    B. A skunk
    C. A bird

2. (5) Where does a gray squirrel live?

    A. In a tree
    B. In the water
    C. In a cave

3. (5) A tree's trunk is:

    A. Underground
    B. At the very top of the tree
    C. In the middle of the tree

4. (5) A turtle has a hard shell and scales to cover its body. A turtle is a:

    A. Bird
    B. Reptile
    C. Mammal

5. (5) A dragonfly is:

    A. A bird
    B. An insect
    C. A lizard

6. (1) Yes/No

    Do all mammals drink milk when they are babies?

Wildlife Challenge – *Junior Edition*©

Answers

---

1. B. A skunk

2. A. In a tree

3. C. In the middle of the tree

4. B. Reptile

5. B. An insect

6. Yes

Wildlife Challenge – *Junior Edition*©

Questions

1. (5) A penguin is a:

   A. Bird
   B. Fish
   C. Mammal

2. (5) A baby deer is called a:

   A. Pup
   B. Fawn
   C. Kitten

3. (5) A lily pad is a flowering plant that grows:

   A. In the water
   B. On a tree
   C. In the desert

4. (5) What do snakes do when the weather turns cold?

   A. They fly south for the winter.
   B. They hibernate in winter dens.
   C. They put on a fur coat.

5. (5) A meadowlark is:

   A. A bird
   B. An insect
   C. A mammal

6. (5) When an animal is hibernating, it is:

   A. Sleeping
   B. Eating
   C. Swimming

Wildlife Challenge – *Junior Edition*©

Answers

1. A. Bird
2. B. Fawn
3. A. In the water
4. B. They hibernate in winter dens.
5. A. A bird
6. A. Sleeping

Wildlife Challenge – *Junior Edition*©

Questions

1. (5) A giraffe:

    A. Has spots
    B. Has stripes
    C. Is solid black

2. (1) A baby fox is called a:

    A. Cub
    B. Fawn
    C. Kit

3. (5) What part of a tree grows in the dirt?

    A. Branches
    B. Trunk
    C. Roots

4. (5) A snake and a lizard are reptiles. A reptile is covered with:

    A. Fur
    B. Scales
    C. Skin

5. (1) Birds have feathers and mammals have fur. What is a chicken – a mammal or a bird?

6. (5) A predator is an animal that lives by hunting and eating other animals. Which of these animals is a predator?

    A. A lion
    B. A cow
    C. A zebra

Wildlife Challenge – *Junior Edition*©

Answers

1. A. Has spots
2. C. Kit
3. C. Roots
4. B. Scales
5. A bird
6. A. A lion

Wildlife Challenge – *Junior Edition*©

Questions

1.   (1)   True/False

All birds, reptiles, and some mammals lay eggs.

2.   (5)   A groundhog or woodchuck eats:

A.   Bugs and insects
B.   Grass and vegetables
C.   Other animals

3.   (5)   A cactus grows:

A.   In a forest
B.   In a desert
C.   At the North Pole

4.   (1)   A frog has moist skin and no claws. A frog is:

A.   An insect
B.   An amphibian
C.   A mammal

5.   (5)   The smallest bird in the world is:

A.   An ostrich
B.   An eagle
C.   A hummingbird

6.   (5)   When the land, water, or air is poisoned with chemical waste or smog, it is:

A.   Endangered
B.   Polluted
C.   Extinct

Wildlife Challenge – *Junior Edition*©

Answers

1. True

2. B. Grass and vegetables

3. B. In a desert

4. B. An amphibian

5. C. A hummingbird

6. B. Polluted

Wildlife Challenge – *Junior Edition*©

Questions

1. (5) How do whales, porpoises, and dolphins breathe?

   A. Through gills
   B. Through a nose
   C. Through a blow hole on top of the head

2. (5) Which one of these animals has a black mask, a ring tail, and sometimes washes its food in the water before eating it?

   A. Beaver
   B. Raccoon
   C. Squirrel

3. (5) Paper is made of:

   A. Coal
   B. Wood
   C. Glass

4. (5) Reptiles do not have fur. They have scales or plates and their toes have claws. Which one of the following is a reptile?

   A. Bear
   B. Crocodile
   C. Crow

5. (5) A duck is a:

   A. Mammal
   B. Reptile
   C. Bird

6. (5) When rushing water moves soil and rock from one place to another, it is called:

   A. Poaching
   B. Erosion
   C. Tropics

Wildlife Challenge – *Junior Edition*©

Answers

1. C.   A blow hole on top of the head
2. B.   A raccoon
3. B.   Wood
4. B.   Crocodile
5. C.   Bird
6. B.   Erosion

Wildlife Challenge – *Junior Edition*©

Questions

1. (5) How does a mother kangaroo carry her baby?

   A. On her back
   B. In a special pouch
   C. In her arms

2. (5) Which one of these animals has very sharp quills all over its body?

   A. Bear
   B. Skunk
   C. Porcupine

3. (5) An acorn is the seed of:

   A. An oak tree
   B. A pine tree
   C. A cactus

4. (5) Alligators and crocodiles live:

   A. In the desert
   B. At the South Pole (Antarctica)
   C. In warm water swamps, lakes, and marshes

5. (5) A honey bee is an insect that produces a sweet syrup that humans like to eat. What is the sweet syrup called?

   A. Honey
   B. Maple syrup
   C. Apple cider

6. (5) The area where an animal lives is called its:

   A. Habitat
   B. Town
   C. Address

Wildlife Challenge – *Junior Edition*©

Answers

1. B.   In a special pouch

2. C.   Porcupine

3. A.   An oak tree

4. C.   In warm water swamps, lakes, and marshes

5. A.   Honey

6. A.   Habitat

Wildlife Challenge – *Junior Edition*©

Questions

1. (5) Where do monkeys build their sleeping nests?

   A. On the ground
   B. In a tree
   C. On a floating tree in the water

2. (5) A baby bear is called a:

   A. Cub
   B. Kitten
   C. Pup

3. (5) A cone is the seed of:

   A. An oak tree
   B. A pine tree
   C. A maple tree

4. (1) Yes/No

   Is a Speckled Kingsnake a poisonous snake?

5. (5) A cricket is:

   A. An insect
   B. A bird
   C. A reptile

6. (5) When a mountain violently erupts, spewing out lava, the mountain is called:

   A. An earthquake
   B. A volcano
   C. A hurricane

Wildlife Challenge – *Junior Edition*©

Answers

1. B. In a tree

2. A. A cub

3. B. A pine tree

4. No

5. A. An insect

6. B. A volcano

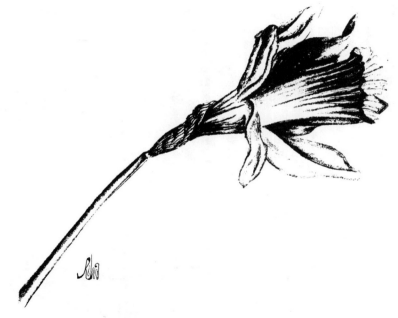

Wildlife Challenge – *Junior Edition*©

Questions

1. (5) An orangutan is:

   A. A bear
   B. An ape
   C. A lion

2. (5) Which animal is the smallest?

   A. Mouse
   B. Rabbit
   C. Raccoon

3. (5) A hole at the top of a dead tree is a good home for a:

   A. Woodpecker, raccoon or squirrel
   B. Deer, rabbit or fox
   C. Fish, moose or turtle

4. (1) True/False

   Turtles lay eggs.

5. (5) A bird that catches and eats small animals is called a bird of prey. The _____ is a bird of prey.

   A. Owl
   B. Cardinal
   C. Pigeon

6. (5) The Arctic (North Pole) is covered with:

   A. Sand
   B. Snow and ice
   C. Large trees and green grass

Wildlife Challenge – *Junior Edition*©

Answers

1. B. An ape
2. A. Mouse
3. A. Bird, raccoon or squirrel
4. True
5. A. Owl
6. B. Snow and ice

Wildlife Challenge – *Junior Edition*©

Questions

1. (1) True/False

   A cheetah can run faster than any other animal on earth.

2. (5) A bobcat and lynx are members of the:

   A. Bird family
   B. Cat family
   C. Dog family (canine)

3. (5) The outer part of a tree trunk is called its:

   A. Leaves
   B. Bark
   C. Roots

4. (1) True/False

   Snakes have legs.

5. (5) Which of these birds does not fly?

   A. Ostrich
   B. Hawk
   C. Owl

6. (1) True/False

   When a squirrel or rabbit has snow white fur and pink eyes, it is called an albino.

Wildlife Challenge – *Junior Edition*©

Answers

1. True

2. B. Cat family

3. B. Bark

4. False

5. A. Ostrich

6. True

Wildlife Challenge – *Junior Edition*

Questions

1. (5) A seal lives in the:

   A. Ocean
   B. Desert
   C. Forest

2. (5) A squirrel likes to eat:

   A. Nuts and fruits
   B. Fish
   C. Grass

3. (5) What time of the year does an oak tree lose its leaves?

   A. Spring
   B. Summer
   C. Fall/Winter

4. (1) Yes/No

   Can a snake swim?

5. (5) Termites are insects that eat:

   A. Grass and leaves
   B. Fruit and vegetables
   C. Wood

6. (1) True/False

   Snow is made out of frozen milk.

Wildlife Challenge – *Junior Edition*©

Answers

1. A. In the ocean
2. A. Nuts and fruits
3. C. Winter
4. Yes
5. C. Wood
6. False

Wildlife Challenge – *Junior Edition*©

Questions

1. (5) A grizzly is a:

    A. Cat
    B. Bear
    C. Bird

2. (1) True/False

    Moose have antlers.

3. (5) Apples and peaches grow:

    A. Underground
    B. On a vine
    C. On a tree

4. (1) True/False

    Snakes can climb to the tops of trees.

5. (5) Which of these birds hunts for mice at night?

    A. A duck
    B. An owl
    C. A pigeon

6. (5) The water in the ocean tastes very:

    A. Sweet
    B. Sour
    C. Salty

Wildlife Challenge – *Junior Edition*©

Answers

1. B. Bear
2. True
3. C. On a tree
4. True
5. B. An owl
6. C. Salty

Wildlife Challenge – *Junior Edition*©

Questions

1. (5) A wolf looks like a:

   A. Big house cat
   B. Big dog
   C. Cow

2. (5) A porcupine is a mammal that has sharp quills and eats tree bark. Where does a porcupine live?

   A. Desert
   B. Underwater
   C. The forests of North America

3. (5) A dandelion is a:

   A. Plant
   B. Animal
   C. Fish

4. (5) A tadpole is a baby:

   A. Frog
   B. Fish
   C. Turtle

5. (5) A swan is a bird that lives in:

   A. The desert
   B. A lake or pond
   C. The forest

6. (5) A fluffy cloud that floats across the sky is made of:

   A. Feathers
   B. Whipped cream
   C. Water

Wildlife Challenge – *Junior Edition*©

Answers

1. B. Big dog
2. C. The forests of North America
3. A. Plant
4. A. Frog
5. B. A lake or pond
6. C. Water

Wildlife Challenge – *Junior Edition*©

Questions

1. (5) A dolphin lives:

   A. In the desert
   B. In the ocean
   C. In the forest

2. (1) True/False

   When a baby fox is born, it is immediately able to see and hear.

3. (5) What is the name of the largest trees in the world?

   A. Oak trees
   B. Peach trees
   C. Giant Sequoia trees

4. (5) A frog eats:

   A. Insects
   B. Grass
   C. Fruits and seeds

5. (5) A vulture is a large bird that eats:

   A. Live fish
   B. Dead animals
   C. Plants

6. (5) On cold mornings, there is a thin covering of ice on the grass and leaves that is called:

   A. Rain
   B. Dew
   C. Frost

129

Wildlife Challenge – *Junior Edition*©

Answers

1. B. In the ocean
2. False
3. C. Giant Sequoia trees
4. A. Insects
5. B. Dead animals
6. C. Frost

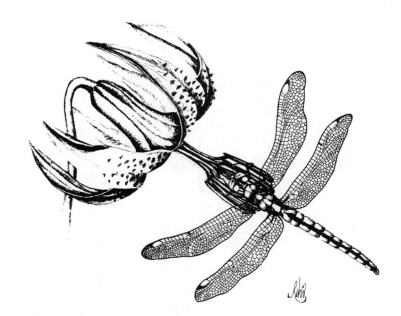

130

Wildlife Challenge – *Junior Edition*©

Questions

1. (5) A whale lives:

   A. In the desert
   B. In the forest
   C. In the ocean

2. (5) A rabbit eats:

   A. Grass, fruits, and vegetables
   B. Small birds
   C. Fish

3. (5) Palm trees grow where the weather is:

   A. Cool all the time
   B. Warm most of the time
   C. Cold all the time

4. (5) A snake's skin feels:

   A. Cool and dry
   B. Warm and wet
   C. Slimy

5. (1) True/False

   A mosquito spends the first part of its life in water.

6. (5) Animals without backbones are called:

   A. Birds
   B. Mammals
   C. Invertebrates

Wildlife Challenge – *Junior Edition*©

Answers

1. C. In the ocean

2. A. Grass, fruits, and vegetables

3. B. Warm most of the time

4. A. Cool and dry

5. True

6. C. Invertebrates

Wildlife Challenge – *Junior Edition*©

Questions

1. (5) What animal can run more than 60 miles an hour for a short time?

   A. An elephant
   B. An anteater
   C. A cheetah

2. (5) The largest North American rodent (an animal that gnaws on wood) is a:

   A. Deer
   B. Beaver
   C. Fox

3. (5) A place where many trees grow together is called:

   A. A parking lot
   B. Forest, woods
   C. Clearcut

4. (5) A turtle lays its eggs in a nest:

   A. In a tree
   B. Underwater
   C. Buried underground

5. (5) The largest living bird is the:

   A. Blackbird
   B. Penguin
   C. Ostrich

6. (5) What is destroying millions of acres of rain forests a year?

   A. Farming and logging
   B. Over-population of animals
   C. Acid rain

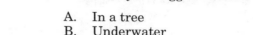

133

Wildlife Challenge – *Junior Edition*©
Answers

1. C. A cheetah

2. B. A beaver

3. B. Forest, woods

4. B. Buried underground

5. C. Ostrich

6. A. Farming and logging

Wildlife Challenge – *Junior Edition*©

Questions

1. (5) What color is a Giant Panda?

   A. Brown
   B. Black and white
   C. Purple

2. (1) True/False

   A squirrel is a rodent and its front teeth grow all the time.

3. (5) The White Oak tree's acorns are a good source of food for:

   A. Deer and squirrels
   B. Fish and snakes
   C. Hawks and owls

4. (5) Snakes eat a large number of:

   A. Fruits and berries
   B. Rodents, birds, and bird eggs
   C. Peanut butter and jelly sandwiches

5. (5) The purple martins are birds that eat a large number of:

   A. Fruits and berries
   B. Small flying insects
   C. Mice and snakes

6. (5) What is a marsupial (Mar-su-pi-al)?

   A. A pouched mammal
   B. A fish
   C. A bird

Wildlife Challenge – *Junior Edition*©

Answers

1. B.   Black and white
2. True
3. A.   Deer and squirrels
4. B.   Rodents, birds, and bird eggs
5. B.   Small flying insects
6. A.   A pouched mammal

Wildlife Challenge – *Junior Edition*©

Questions

1. (5) What color is a zebra?

   A. Brown and gray
   B. Black and white
   C. Solid black

2. (5) What animal is a rodent that cuts down big trees with its large, orange teeth?

   A. A squirrel
   B. A beaver
   C. A bear

3. (1) True/False

   Cedar, pine and spruce trees are called evergreens because they stay green during the cold, winter months.

4. (5) A frog is an amphibian (am-FIB-ee-un) that calls to its mate by:

   A. Barking
   B. Whining
   C. Croaking

5. (5) Eagles, hawks and owls are birds of prey that have powerful talons (Tal-ons) on their:

   A. Wings
   B. Feet
   C. Head

6. (5) An animal that eats the flesh of dead animals is called a:

   A. Gizzard
   B. Scavenger (Sca-ven-ger)
   C. Reptile

Wildlife Challenge – *Junior Edition*©

Answers

1. B. Black and white
2. B. A beaver
3. True
4. C. Croaking
5. B. Feet
6. B. Scavenger

Wildlife Challenge – *Junior Edition*©

Questions

1. (5) The black and white Killer Whale eats:

    A. Fruits and vegetables
    B. Seals and penguins
    C. Insects

2. (5) When frightened or hurt, an opossum will:

    A. Play dead
    B. Run
    C. Attack

3. (5) Kelp is a plant that grows:

    A. In the desert
    B. On a mountain
    C. In the ocean

4. (5) Baby frogs and toads (tadpoles) have:

    A. Large teeth
    B. Gills and tails
    C. Feathers

5. (5) When a bird flies south for the winter it is:

    A. Migrating (Mi-grat-ing)
    B. Diurnal (Di-urn-al)
    C. Nocturnal (Noc-turn-al)

6. (5) Which of the following is a mammal?

    A. Dog
    B. Frog
    C. Snake

139

Wildlife Challenge – *Junior Edition*©

Answers

1. B.   Seals and penguins
2. A.   Play dead
3. C.   In the ocean
4. B.   Gills and tails
5. A.   Migrating
6. A.   Dog

Wildlife Challenge – *Junior Edition*©

Questions

1. (5) A North American porcupine eats:

   A. Other animals
   B. Twigs, leaves and buds
   C. Nuts and berries

2. (5) A mole lives:

   A. In the water
   B. Underground
   C. In trees

3. (5) Algae (Al-jee) are simple plants that grow:

   A. On rocks
   B. In dirt
   C. In water

4. (1) True/False

   Snakes eat frogs.

5. (5) Flies are:

   A. Mammals
   B. Insects
   C. Reptiles

6. (5) Dry land where very little rain falls is called:

   A. An oasis (O-a-sis)
   B. A desert
   C. A forest

Answers

1. B. Twigs, leaves and buds
2. B. Underground
3. C. In water
4. True
5. B. Insects
6. B. A desert

Wildlife Challenge – *Junior Edition*©

Questions

1. (1) True/False

   A large grizzly bear has a very short tail.

2. (5) A lynx is a large bobtailed:

   A. Cat
   B. Deer
   C. Bear

3. (5) Which vegetable grows underground?

   A. A tomato
   B. Corn
   C. A potato

4. (5) Toads and frogs eat:

   A. Leaves and seeds
   B. Insects, invertebrates, and some small birds.
   C. Flowers

5. (5) A dragonfly is:

   A. A dragon
   B. An insect
   C. A bird

6. (5) A place where a bird sleeps at night is called a:

   A. Bed
   B. Roost
   C. Clutch

143

Wildlife Challenge – *Junior Edition*©

Answers

1. True

2. A. Cat

3. C. A potato

4. B. Insects, invertebrates, and some small birds.

5. B. An insect

6. B. Roost

Wildlife Challenge – *Junior Edition*©

Questions

1. (1) True/False

   Worms have a backbone.

2. (5) A female opossum carries her babies in a pouch. An animal with a pouch is called a:

   A. Marsupial (Mar-sup-i-al)
   B. Bird
   C. Dirunal (Di-ur-nal)

3. (5) The yellow powder in the center of flowers is called:

   A. Dust
   B. Pollen
   C. Seeds

4. (5) An alligator eats:

   A. Fruit
   B. Other animals
   C. Vegetables

5. (5) A bald eagle is a:

   A. Deer
   B. Fish
   C. Bird

6. (5) A tornado is a large, dangerous cloud that is shaped like a:

   A. Funnel
   B. Ball
   C. Disk

Wildlife Challenge – *Junior Edition*©

Answers

1. False

2. A. Marsupial

3. B. Pollen

4. B. Other animals

5. C. Bird

6. A. Funnel

Wildlife Challenge – *Junior Edition*©

Questions

1. (5) A leopard is a very large animal that is a member of the:

   A. Rodent family
   B. Cat family
   C. Bird family

2. (5) An otter is an animal that lives:

   A. Around water
   B. In the desert
   C. In the top of a tree

3. (5) When you eat lettuce, you are eating the plant's:

   A. Flowers
   B. Roots
   C. Leaves

4. (1) Yes/No

   Does a frog have webbed feet?

5. (5) An osprey is a bird that eats:

   A. Fish
   B. Nuts and seeds
   C. Large animals

6. (5) Silk fabric is made from:

   A. A caterpillar's cocoon
   B. Sheep wool
   C. Rabbit fur

147

Wildlife Challenge – *Junior Edition*©

Answers

1. B. Cat family

2. A. Around water

3. C. Leaves

4. Yes

5. A. Fish

6. A. A caterpillar's cocoon

Wildlife Challenge – *Junior Edition*©

Questions

1. (1) True/False

   Chimpanzees cannot swim.

2. (5) Which of these animals does not have large tusks?

   A. A raccoon
   B. A walrus
   C. An elephant

3. (5) What part of the plant do you eat when eating a carrot or an onion?

   A. The stem
   B. The root
   C. The leaves

4. (5) A tree frog climbs a tree by using:

   A. Its large claws
   B. The suction cups on its feet
   C. A ladder

5. (5) When a bird is preening (Preen-ing), it is:

   A. Gathering food
   B. Cleaning its feathers
   C. Building a nest

6. (5) A group of cattle is called a herd. A group of wolves is called a pack. What is a group of birds called?

   A. Flock
   B. School
   C. Pride

Wildlife Challenge – *Junior Edition*©

Answers

1. True

2. A. A raccoon

3. B. The root

4. B. The suction cups on its feet

5. B. Cleaning its feathers

6. A. Flock

Wildlife Challenge©

GAME RULES

Object of the Game:

The object of the game is to gain as many points as possible to win the game. The player who fills all the categories does not necessarily win, although the player or player teams who completes all the categories on their scorecard will add 5 bonus points to their score.

Number of Players:

Two to twenty people can play. Can be played with individual players or in teams of two or more.

How to Begin:

1. One or more designated readers may read the questions. The page must be turned after each question is read and answered.

2. Each player rolls the numeral die and the highest number rolled goes first.

3. All True/False and Yes/No questions are worth 1 point.

4. All multiple choice questions are worth 5 points.

5. If either multiple choice, True/False, or Yes/No questions are answered incorrectly, the score will be zero in that category.

6. Category is determined by the number on the die. Example: If you roll three on the die, you will answer Question No. 3 in the game book.

7. Only True/False questions can be passed. Multiple choice questions and Yes/No questions must be answered by the player rolling the die.

8. An incorrectly answered question is the only reason to enter a zero in the category. If you miss a turn or have used up your space, you do not place a zero in any of the categories.

Example	Score Pad			TOTAL
1	5	1	0	6
2	0	0	5	5
3	1	1		2
4	5	0	0	5
5	1	0	5	6
6	0	5	5	10

TOTAL SCORE ___34___

Wildlife Challenge©

GAME RULES, Continued

As the game progresses, certain categories on your scorecard will fill. For example, if Categories 1, 4, 5 and 6 are filled on your scorecard, you must roll a 2 or 3 to play. If you roll a 4 and get a True/False question, you may pass it to the next person and have a chance at another roll. If that player's card is full in Category 4, the player who originally rolled the 4 must miss his turn. This process continues until a player completely fills all categories on his scorecard. The winner will be determined by the player or team of players having the most points.

About True/False Questions:

- True/False questions can be answered or passed to the person to the immediate left of the player.

- The decision whether to take or pass the question must be made before the question is read.

- If the player chooses not to pass the question, he must then answer it. If the player passes the question, at that time the player he passed to must answer the question correctly or take a zero in that category.

- If the person who originally drew the True/False question incorrectly answers the question, then he must take a zero in that specified category and the game will continue to the next player.

- If the True/False question is passed, the player who passed the True/False question is then able to roll the die again and hope to get a multiple choice question worth 5 points.

- If this player rolls a second True/False question instead of a multiple choice, he has to answer it correctly or take a zero in the category.

- At this time, the player that answered the True/False question will be skipped and the next player will roll the die. This will continue around the table until all spaces are filled on each card.

Wildlife Challenge Junior©

If young children are playing with adults, they will use the questions in Wildlife Challenge Junior©. If younger players are passed a True/False question, take the question from the Junior Edition. If younger players pass a True/False question to an adult, take the question from Wildlife Challenge© in the same category. The rules for both editions are the same.

Wildlife Challenge®

Glossary

Amphibian: An animal that breathes through gills and lives in water while young; as an adult, lives primarily on land and breathes through lungs and moist, glandular skin.
EXAMPLE: Frogs, toads, and skinks.

Annual: A seed-bearing plant that completes its life cycle from seedling to maturity during a single growing season.
EXAMPLE: Tomato, squash, petunia, and corn.

Aquatic: Growing, living, or frequenting water.
EXAMPLE: A fish is an aquatic animal; a water lily is an aquatic plant.

Biodegradable: A substance that is broken down by microorganisms into simple, stable matter.
EXAMPLE: Paper, wood, and cloth are biodegradable. Glass, heavy plastics, and aluminum cans are not biodegradable.

Carnivore: An animal or plant that eats meat to survive.
EXAMPLE: A dog, cat, tiger, wolf, owl, and hawk are carnivores.

Carrion: Decaying bodies of dead animals.
EXAMPLE: A buzzard eats the carcass (carrion) of an opossum that was killed by a car.

Compost: A mixture of decomposed vegetable matter.
EXAMPLE: When leaves, vegetable waste, and soil are combined and allowed to decompose, the organic material produced is compost.

Conifer: A plant that bears its seeds in cones.
EXAMPLE: Pine trees are conifers.

Conservation: The wise and intelligent use or protection of natural resources.
EXAMPLE: When a tree is cut for lumber, as a good conservation effort, another tree should be planted in its place.

Deciduous: Broad-leaved trees (such as maples and oaks) that shed their leaves before winter.
EXAMPLE: An oak tree is classified as deciduous because it sheds its leaves in the late fall and grows new leaves in the spring.

Wildlife Challenge®

Glossary

Decomposer: A plant or animal that feeds on dead material and causes its mechanical or chemical breakdown.
EXAMPLE: Some types of fungi and molds are decomposers because they live off decaying matter.

Desert: Environments with very little rainfall.
EXAMPLE: The Mojave Desert of California and the Arabian Desert of Egypt.

Diurnal: Active during daylight hours.
EXAMPLE: Sparrows, gray squirrels, and chipmunks sleep at night and are active during the day.

Earthquake: A shaking or trembling of the earth caused by volcanic activity or shifting of the earth's crust along a fault line.
EXAMPLE: The earthquakes along the San Andreas fault of California and East coast earthquakes along the New Madrid fault.

Endangered: A plant or animal that is in danger of becoming extinct.
EXAMPLE: Because of loss of habitat, the Florida Panther is considered an endangered species.

Environment: The surroundings of a plant or animal.
EXAMPLE: A fish must live in an aquatic (water) environment.

Extinct: A plant or animal that is no longer in existence.
EXAMPLE: Dinosaurs, passenger pigeons, and dodo birds are extinct.

Feral: Domesticated animals that survive in the wild.
EXAMPLE: Dogs, cats, pigs, and goats that have escaped human captivity and are surviving on their own.

Wildlife Challenge®

Glossary

Forest: A complex community of plants and animals in which trees are most numerous. EXAMPLE: The forest is made up of oak, pine, spruce, and elm trees which provide food and shelter for a number of different animals.

Habitat: The combination of food, water, and shelter necessary for a plant or animal to survive. EXAMPLE: A deer must have plenty of grass to eat, water to drink, and shelter from predators and the elements.

Herbivore: An animal that eats only plants. EXAMPLE: A giraffe, cow, zebra, and sheep are herbivores.

Hibernation: A state of sleep during the cold, winter months. EXAMPLE: The ground hog, chipmunk, and snake hibernate until spring.

Insectivore: An animal that eats insects. EXAMPLE: Anteaters' and armadillos' main diet consists of ants, bugs, and grubs.

Mammal: Warm-blooded vertebrates that produce milk to feed their young. EXAMPLE: A human, tiger, elephant, dog, monkey, whale, and seal are mammals

Marsh: A track of low, treeless wetland that supports an abundance of water grasses and wildlife. EXAMPLE: Cattails, lily pads, and sedges are aquatic plants that grow in a marsh.

Migration: Traveling distances because of seasonal changes. EXAMPLE: A herd of caribou migrate south in the spring to feed on the tender vegetation of the tundra.

Nocturnal: Active at night. EXAMPLE: An owl, beaver, and flying squirrel are active mainly at night.

Omnivore: An animal that eats both plants and animals. EXAMPLE: A human, raccoon, opossum, and bear eat plants and animals.

Wildlife Challenge®

Glossary

Pelt: The skin of a fur-bearer.
EXAMPLE: Beaver, raccoons, mink, and rabbit pelts are used to make coats and hats.

Perennial: A plant that survives several years and produces seeds each year.
EXAMPLE: Blackberries, blueberries, and grapes are perennials.

Poaching: The illegal act of killing animals.
EXAMPLE: Elephants are being poached for their ivory tusks.

Pollution: A harmful substance deposited into the air, water, or land that is hazardous to plants and animals.
EXAMPLE: Emissions from cars cause major pollution.

Predator: An animal that kills and eats other animals.
EXAMPLE: A bobcat chases and kills a rabbit. The bobcat is the predator and the rabbit is the prey.

Prey: An animal that is killed and eaten by a predator.
EXAMPLE: An owl caught a mouse with its strong talons. The owl is the predator and the mouse is the prey.

Raptor: Birds which are predatory.
EXAMPLE: Eagles, hawks, owls, and falcons are all raptors (birds of prey).

Reptile: Cold-blooded animals that have either scales, shields, or plates, and their toes have claws.
EXAMPLE: Lizards, turtles, snakes, and crocodiles are reptiles.

Scavenger: An animal that feeds on waste and dead animals.
EXAMPLE: Buzzards, dung beetles, and maggots are scavengers.

Swamp: A tract of land covered with shallow water that supports a variety of wildlife and bottomland hardwood.
EXAMPLE: Giant cypress trees grace the swamps of the Southeastern United States.

Wildlife Challenge®

Glossary

Tornado:	A violent and destructive whirlwind. EXAMPLE: A violent thunderstorm may produce lightning, hail, rain, or tornadoes
Volcano:	A vent in the earth's crust that allows pressure to be released in the form of molten rock and steam. EXAMPLE: Mount St. Helen's was a dormant volcano that erupted in Washington State in the 1980s.
Venom:	The poison of snakes and spiders. EXAMPLE: A rattlesnake injects poisonous venom into its prey with long, hollow fangs.

To order additional books of Wildlife Challenge or large quantities of books at a reduced price, contact your local bookstore or:

Wildlife Challenge
P.O. Box 175
Roland, Arkansas 72135

August House Publishing
P.O. Box 3223
Little Rock, Arkansas 72203
Phone 1-800-284-8784